INVERCLYDE

Matador
9 Priory Business Park,
Wistow Road, Kibworth Beauchamp,
Leicestershire. LE8 0RX
Tel: 0116 279 2299
Email: books@troubador.co.uk
Web: www.troubador.co.uk/matador
Twitter: @matadorbooks

ISBN 978 1789013 771

British Library Cataloguing in Publication Data.
A catalogue record for this book is available from the British Library.

Printed and bound by CPI Group (UK) Ltd, Croydon CR0 4YY
Typeset in 11pt Minion Pro by Troubador Publishing Ltd, Leicester, UK

Matador is an imprint of Troubador Publishing Ltd

To the dog-walkers of Norwich, without whom Hector almost certainly would have met an unhappy end.

Thank you for your help and encouraging me to tell Hector's story.

CONTENTS

Foreword

"I've asked all my colleagues," said Jacquie our dog trainer friend, "and the opinion is unanimous – DON'T GET A BEAGLE. They're disobedient, untrainable, stubborn, greedy, just plain naughty!" Well, that's as may be, but our minds had already been made up. Yes, there is no denying that beagles are all of those things, but they are also very loving and gentle, with a great sense of fun and adventure. The search was on for a puppy – in our family the opinion was also unanimous – we loved beagles and it was a beagle and only a beagle that would be our first family dog.

Reggie was an adorable puppy, a classic beagle in every way and we loved him instantly. Reggie enjoyed his first three years as an 'only dog', then one day things were to change forever…

A true account, featuring real dogs and people.

A Disabled Beagle Puppy

It really was all Beagle-Emma's fault. Long-term beagle owner and self-confessed beagle obsessive, Emma was on the hunt for another beagle. "I've promised the boys a puppy," she said. Roxy, their current beagle-in-residence, had been a rescue from a dogs' home and came to them at around five or six years old (no one really knew) after Beagle Rolo had passed away. "You see, they've never actually had a beagle *puppy*," she went on.

After many visits to breeders, Emma found little Bo, who was put on order for collection at twelve weeks old. Amid the great excitement, a rather disturbing issue came to light. Emma came straight out with it, "In Bo's litter, there's a little boy puppy with only three legs. He's going to a dogs' home – the breeder has already arranged it." When you are a beagle's human, you automatically love all beagles, and I imagine that this is similar for all other breeds too. I had a terrible mental image of a little disabled

1

puppy living in a cage for the rest of his life, with no one to love him.

Beagle-Emma went on, "Do you think Reggie might like a friend? It's really hardly any more trouble to have two dogs when you already have one…" I had heard this said on several occasions, that two dogs were double the pleasure, but not double the effort, but I wasn't completely convinced. I said I would discuss it with my husband James (also fanatical about beagles, but generally sensible otherwise). On the way home, I could think of nothing else – Head: I am time-poor, with almost zero capacity for taking anything else on. Heart: we have to give him a home and look after him – he's disabled and needs all the looking-after he can get. I talked it over with the children that evening – of course, they were in unusual and immediate agreement – we must have him – there was no question – their minds were made up in a split second. In terms of the heart, there was absolutely no hesitation; it was the head that was the problem – the niggling practicalities of taking on this puppy, and the extra complications that his disability might bring. How would I manage a disabled dog on top of looking after three children and another full-on beagle, not to mention running my own business and the household virtually on my own as James worked abroad most of the time? The children all promised to help (where had I heard that before? Ah yes, when we were getting Reggie – "We'll walk and feed him," they had all clamoured…).

Things were a little easier now that the children were older, I told myself – Ellie was nearly fifteen, Max thirteen and Freddy nine – at least they didn't need quite as much looking after as they had done as babies and toddlers.

It had taken a good couple of years to make the life-changing decision to get a dog – and change our life it certainly did! The sturdiest, most inquisitive and nosiest puppy of the litter, Reggie was a larger-than-life character from the start. Since beagles have a reputation for picking up a scent and following it to the ends of the earth, some owners never let them off the lead for fear of their never coming back. We were confident that we would be able to train Reggie and it is perhaps this over-confidence that has led to so many beagle adventures (much more of this later). Beagles are absolutely adorable, with huge characters, but our dog-trainer-friend Jacquie and her colleagues were absolutely right – beagles just do their own thing, which is more often than not food-related. Once you have accepted this, life as a beagle owner becomes more straightforward.

We had persisted with letting Reggie off the lead and often came home with a tale to tell – walks were rarely incident-free. A lady who was training her young dog in the park had a plastic bag full of freshly cooked liver to give to her puppy as a very special treat for returning to her. Reggie smelled the liver from over a hundred metres away, locked his sights, started his final approach from about fifty metres, and literally in one fell swoop, without breaking his stride in the slightest, leapt into the air, grabbing the entire bag out of the lady's hand. Before anyone knew what had happened, Reggie had wolfed down the whole lot, plastic bag and all.

On the occasion of Reggie's very first Christmas, such was the lure of the remaining two-thirds of the turkey sitting on the kitchen table, that little Reggie silently managed to wrestle it to the ground and ate what must have been twice his own body weight of Christmas turkey. We came in to find both puppy and the now mostly eaten turkey lying side by side on the floor, Reggie having alerted us to his painful tummy with pitiful little yips as if to say, "Please take the turkey away from me!" In the evening, while we were all arguing over Trivial Pursuit, baby Reggie, having managed to digest the turkey, carefully unwrapped eighteen Cointreau liqueur chocolates and devoured the lot, after which I really think he felt quite bad. Christmas is a great hunting ground for beagles.

Reggie fitted in perfectly with our, at best, slightly hectic and, at worst, totally manic family life, but could we manage another beagle with all their beagley characteristics?

✽

The next morning, I discussed the burning issue of the week with my regular dog-walking friends, both of whom are referred to by their dogs' names as well as their own – partly for clarity when recounting endless dog-walking related adventures (Emma-Amber is not to be confused with Beagle-Emma, for example) and partly for my own amusement.

Emma-Amber (Amber: a pretty, lady-like sheltie) and Katie-Jango (Jango: a hairy wheaten terrier, often mistaken for a cockapoo) listened to the for and against and by the end of the walk had persuaded me that it was definitely the right thing to do and had offered to help where they could with the disabled puppy. Whilst in deep discussion, I had, of course, lost track of Reggie, who had beagled off across the park and into the woods beyond the pitch-and-putt golf course. We spent the next half-hour or so doubling back and searching – eventually, Emma-Amber spotting the flag-like white tail tip zig-zagging through the trees. Then, with little or no thought for his own personal safety as high-speed golf balls whizzed past his generous ears, or for slightly grumpy looking golfers, he shot across three greens and rejoined us, panting happily and hoping for a biscuit.

1

I had elected not to mention it to James by email or phone while he was working away in Romania that week. Today was Thursday and he was due home that evening – I was very conscious that the clock was ticking. If we didn't take action, the puppy would be sent to the home. I had been living with the issue for several days, and in my view it had now become urgent. It was, of course, a completely new subject for James, but I thought it best just to dive right in and get straight to the point: "There's a three-legged beagle puppy who is going to go into a dogs' home and live in a cage…"

He interrupted me. "We'll have him," he said calmly and firmly. So the decision was made. "We'll call him Hector," he went on, "after Hector of Troy – the bravest of the brave."

Relieved that the decision was made, I told the children the good news, and the household was lifted by a frisson of excitement. Discussing it later that evening, James pointed out that it would be good for the children to understand that not everything is perfect in life – not every person or dog is fully able-bodied and this is something with which we should come to terms. The 2012 Paralympics in London had taught many of us to view people with disabilities in a totally different way; not only to be accepting of people who are less able than we are, but to understand what incredible things people can achieve.

I contacted the breeder and she was delighted that we were going to give the puppy a home. I then started to do a bit of research into dogs with missing or disabled front legs and found out some interesting and useful facts – such as dogs carry around sixty per cent of their weight on their front legs, so it was worse for Hector that he had a front disabled leg, rather than a back one. The breeder explained that the leg wasn't actually missing but was withered and hadn't grown like the others. She mentioned that it could be beneficial to amputate the withered leg, as it might get in his way and added to Hector's overall weight, which should be kept to a minimum, since it had to be carried by only three legs.

The idea that we would have to keep his weight down came as a bit of a shock! Beagles are notoriously greedy and tend to pile on the pounds. I spoke to our vet about it and about how the lack of a leg might affect other aspects such as the spine and the other legs, but in the end we concluded that there was no real point in speculating about what may or may not be the effects of Hector's disability – it is what it is.

*

It was late February when we drove the eighty miles or so through proper snowdrifts to visit the beagle puppy. The puppies were about six weeks old and completely adorable as all beagle puppies are, in fact, as absolutely all puppies are. The disabled puppy rolled and played with the others, hopping about excitedly, nibbling our fingers and shoelaces and hopping onto Ellie's lap. There is no bone in Hector's front left leg; it isn't at all weight-bearing. He tucks it up under his chest, and it isn't really very noticeable until he starts to move about. We loved him with no hesitation or reservation.

Bo and Hector would be ready for collection in April, and since we were away on holiday on the appointed date, a Puppy Collection Plan was put in motion. Beagle-Emma and family collected both puppies and looked after them for the first four days until we got home. This turned out to be the best possible way of taking a puppy away from his or her mother. Hector and Bo had each other, they rousted about all day, snuggling up in the same tiny puppy bed in 'ying and yang' positions when exhaustion struck, which it often did.

The situation was so perfect, in fact, that we worried about how to handle it when we got back from holiday, and so a Puppy Transfer Plan was hatched. Hector and his sister came to our house for a few hours each day for Hector to acclimatise, and for a good couple of weeks, we arranged for them to have regular play dates at each other's houses. Both puppies settled in to their own families and each was lucky enough to have a beagle role model – Roxy was Bo's mother figure, whereas Reggie was more of a teenage older brother to Hector, not nearly as responsible or sensible and leading the way when it came to beagle badness.

The issue of where the new baby puppy should sleep had been discussed while we were away, and we came to the conclusion that he should sleep on Ellie's bed. This was a slightly risky plan in terms of toileting during the night, but we felt it was the best option – I'm not sure if Ellie fully agreed as she endured nights with the squirming, sharp-clawed little Hector. After a few days, though, we thought he would be ready to sleep with Reggie, now known as the Big Beagle.

TWO

Reggie and Little Hec

Poor Reggie. He is the most intuitive dog I've ever known – he instinctively knows which human is going to walk him as soon as we've decided ourselves. He can tell the difference between 'smart' trainers and dog-walking trainers and starts to bark in a very loud, monotonous and continuous fashion until the shoes are laced up, the poo bags are in the pocket and the lead is taken off the hook near the back door.

Reggie considers all dogs and people to be his friends, and we didn't have a moment's worry about introducing a new puppy into the household. Super-intuitive he may be, but there was still no way of preparing Reggie for a new baby in the house; we weren't able to buy him a *When Puppy Comes Home* book and give him a present as you would the firstborn child in a family. Reggie would just have to cope.

As expected, Reg took it in his stride and from the outset Little Hec looked to Reg for guidance, snuggling up to him at nap-time. There has never been any doubt that Reggie is actually Hector's master, rather than any human members of the family. As is always the case with the arrival of a new puppy, the joy and excitement is tempered by the little parcels and pools left around the house, and we soon understood that Hector wasn't a particularly fast learner. Hector comes from a very distinguished line of pedigree beagles and has quite an aristocratic look about him, with fine features and beautiful tricolour beagle markings, but he certainly wasn't the sharpest knife in the drawer – it was a good many months before he learned his own name!

While little Bo up the road was undergoing training from *The Beagle Handbook*, we didn't really try very hard with Hector. Every time he did anything wrong, we would smile and say, "He's only a puppy and he's disabled, never mind!" Eventually, Hector learned that doggy-going-to-the-loo happened outside, but other classic puppy training we decided was inappropriate for Little Hec. He couldn't really balance very well in a sitting position, so we weren't going to teach him to sit; and if we ever wanted him to come, we would go and pick him up and carry him like a baby, to save his 'good legs'. And so Hector became a lap-beagle. While working at my computer during the day, he comes and curls up on my lap, often with his little beagle snout on the keyboard, and in the evening he hops up onto someone's lap to watch the TV, barking fiercely if any dogs appear on the screen.

Sometimes Hector's lack of training had more serious consequences than a puddle on the carpet. Sandy is a well-travelled brown teddy, owned and much loved since birth by Freddy. Sandy has been on every family holiday or short trip and is so protected by his rather absent-minded owner that he has never been lost or damaged and looked rather good for his advancing years.

One day, a truly terrible thing happened: Sandy got in the way of a very chewy young Hector. At teatime, Freddy walked quietly into the kitchen, holding Sandy, something that at the age of nine, he wasn't in the habit of doing. Sandy normally stayed in bed all day and was Freddy's night-time companion. He said in a very small voice, "I think Sandy has been attacked by Hector." This was such a serious offence that there was no shouting or screaming, there were no tears, just a quiet sense of loss.

I rushed over exclaiming, "Oh no, Freddy; I'm so sorry – that's awful…"

Little Hec, however, simply could do no wrong and Freddy replied, "I think he can be mended – we can get him some more eyes and sew them on."

Hector had carefully turned his tiny razor-sharp teeth on Sandy's button eyes, almost gnawing them off completely and making a hole, from which the white fluffy stuffing was seeping out. It was a very sorry sight.

*

The next day, Granny and Grandpa rushed out to a craft shop and bought a bag of teddy bear eyes. With great care, Granny pushed the stuffing back inside and sewed a pair of the new eyes over what remained of the original ones. She did a great job, but the eyes were totally different, the kind that roll around, making Sandy look quite bizarre, almost demented and nothing like the real Sandy. Granny had propped the mended bear up on the counter in the kitchen so that Freddy would see him the minute he got home from school; he ran in, excited by the news that Sandy was all better. The sight of the new Sandy stopped Freddy in his tracks. He said, "But that looks nothing like Sandy – take them off, Granny, take them off!"

Granny unpicked the roving eyes and Sandy was back to his old self – well, almost. We all agreed that the chewed eyes were far preferable to the crazy ones. Freddy accepted that Sandy was Sandy despite Hector's attack and all was well in his world again. Freddy had instantly understood, without anyone needing to explain to him, that puppies have no understanding whatsoever of sacred possessions and, while he would never, ever leave Sandy in a place where a young dog might come across him again, he understands that it is his responsibility to prevent such things from happening and not the dog's fault.

⭐

Walking both dogs together was clearly going to be a challenge – how on earth was Hector going to manage? Reggie, like most beagles, requires and demands miles of walking off the lead every day and it didn't seem possible that Hector would be able to do the same. When Hector was old enough to go out, we walked to the park, Hector happily hopping along on the lead next to Reggie. Once safely in the middle of the park, the furthest distance from any exits, I would set them free, and Hector ran gamely with Reggie, chasing imaginary (and sometimes real) rabbits and would then lie down on the grass and rest for a short while before gambling off again.

Hector became a Very Well-Known Local Dog. Concerned fellow dog walkers would hurry up to us and say, "I think your dog has hurt his leg." Several people picked him up and ran over, saying, "Your dog's wounded – maybe he's been run over?" Every dog walker noticed Hector, and I would watch while they looked worriedly at Little Hec merrily hopping along, saying to each other, "Look at that poor little dog – he's really injured. She's not even looking – do you think she's noticed? I'm going to say something…" And as they reached me: "Excuse me, do you know that your dog is injured?"

And so each and every time I would explain, "It's okay; he was born like that – he's disabled." Invariably, a conversation would follow and I realised that there are very few dogs about who are actually born with a disability – in fact, Hector was the only one I knew, and this is what made him such an interesting little fellow to everyone who set eyes on him.

Hector's disability, coupled with an exceptionally high cute-factor, attracted so much interest that I often felt I should make flyers to hand out to people to tell Hector's story. People are so interested in Hector and comments such as, "We were talking about Hector around the dinner table the other evening," or "So *this* is Hector! I'm so glad to meet him finally!" were commonplace.

Hector developed a special hunting cry, reserved for racing through the undergrowth with Reggie on the scent of a squirrel or fox, or even a deer. It is the most piercing, high-pitched yelping, which rattles your eardrums from five hundred metres and sounds a bit like a very squeaky wheel on an ancient bike, amplified a hundred times. For Hector, running at speed seemed actually easier than going at walking pace – he would get into a rhythm and race along, flying across the long grass. So Hec would do his 'squeaky wheel' in full flight and in full cry, teeth set and nostrils stretched wide – *Once more unto the breach, dear beagles, once more...* while hurtling through the park. Most people in the park, whether they were walking the dog, cycling, skateboarding or sailing a boat on the model boating lake, had certainly never seen or heard anything like it. The sight and sound of Hector caused all manner of distress to passing park-goers, who would eventually identify us as the owners and ask us what was wrong with the poor, limping, shrieking beagle.

When Hector seemed too tired, I would pick him up and carry him for the rest of the walk. This was a challenge when walking back from the park with a badly trained older beagle pulling on the lead, straining to sniff every blade of grass and to snuffle in every discarded crisp packet or sweet wrapper. Until Hector was around six months old, it was fairly manageable, but beagles are stocky creatures and Hector is certainly all beagle. Hector grew and filled out, and while he is a much smaller model of beagle than Reggie, he became quite hefty and increasingly more difficult to carry home. There was no question of leaving him behind, though; he certainly wouldn't have liked that, and the thought of him home alone, crying and whimpering for Reggie, ruled that out completely. Anyhow, a dog needs his walk.

As we watched Hector grow, we became more and more worried about his 'good leg', that is to say, his other front leg, which has to take so much of the strain. It soon became clear that not only was Hector's 'good leg' becoming super-strong since it had to bear so much weight, but it was also not a perfect leg in the first place. So we had to try to think of solutions for taking Hector out. The first idea was a very supportive harness – we would keep him on the lead, maintaining a constant, gentle upward pull to try to give him some support, thereby taking some of the weight off the leg. We tried six, maybe seven different harnesses, and they didn't make any significant difference. In any case, Hector was desperate to go off on adventures with Reg and didn't think much of being kept on a lead, which is fair enough. So we gave up with the harnesses.

By now, I was really struggling to carry him home – it was becoming impossible. Carrying a dog is nothing like carrying a child – dogs don't cling on and are therefore a dead weight. I would huff and puff along the pavement, being pulled in all directions by Reg, who really wasn't tuned in to the situation. A baby's buggy – it came to me in a flash. I will take a buggy with me (we had an old foldaway stroller in the garage) and when Little Hec is tired, I'll pop him in and wheel him home.

Hector didn't like the buggy. He didn't understand why on earth I wanted to put him in there, but he eventually learned that he would get a treat for sitting still, and this method worked well for a while. It meant that I looked even more bizarre, pushing an empty buggy to the park, with a badly behaved, pulling beagle on one side and a disabled one on the other, and on the way back pushing a perfectly healthy looking young beagle in a buggy (you couldn't notice his disability when tucked up in the buggy). A pushchair wasn't a long-term solution, however. It was clear that Hector's situation was going to worsen as he reached full size and got heavier and heavier, and we needed to come up with something that would help preserve his 'good leg' and give him the freedom to do what he loves best – to hurtle round with Reggie.

As Hector was growing up, the bond between us – Hector and his human family – was growing stronger and stronger. We understood different types of woofing, just as we could have a good stab at guessing his mood by the look in his eyes. The relationship between two dogs is a little different. Reggie had accepted Hector as a non-threatening baby animal into his home instantly and without any strings attached. However, dogs are pack animals and there is always a leader, even in a pack of two. Reggie had started off as the natural leader; not only is he the senior dog by some years, he is also a fully able-bodied dog and a much larger beagle, so his leadership went undisputed.

Now that Hector was a fully grown adult dog, things started to change. We noticed how it was always Hector who would win a toy in a play fight. Not only did he have the confidence and the pluck to do it, but he had developed a style of defence which was difficult to penetrate. Once Hector had managed to grab the squeaky pheasant or the red plastic bone, he would turn so that his back was always towards Reg, not unlike a footballer turning to defend the ball. In fact, when the family goes to Carrow Road to watch Norwich City FC, a new meaning for the verb 'to hector' has been thought up: "That was a fantastic bit of hectoring in midfield!" When Reggie managed to get around to the head end, Hector would turn again, shoulder barging him out of the way. All Reggie can think of doing in this situation is to bark – loudly, furiously and endlessly until it goes right through to your bones.

As Hector matured, his personality became more extreme. For our beagles, something like a dried pig's ear is possibly the most special item they could ever possess; and as such, despite their incredible greed, it is to be savoured, played with and, in Hector's case, used in psychological warfare. For anything this special, Reggie's routine is to play with it initially – he picks it up and throws it to you, you throw it back and so the game continues until eventually, after maybe five or six minutes, he will eat it up. Hector, on the other hand, becomes almost demonic in these situations. He can keep a pig's ear for up to about a week, sometimes hiding it in someone's bed and other times laying the precious treasure in a prominent position – in the kitchen doorway, for example – and lying on guard next to it. If Reggie dares approach, there is a deep growl from the back of Hector's throat, accompanied by a look that could turn to stone.

Reggie, on the other hand, was becoming more and more like a person. When the PTA committee came for a meeting, Reggie would join us at the dining room table, sitting neatly on a leather chair, looking every bit a part of the discussion about the school quiz evening as anyone else. Only when the snacks came out would we have to ask him to leave, or he would no doubt suffer from a complete lack of self-control and would snaffle them up in a *Fantastic Mr Fox*-like frenzy.

The dining room has a bay window facing out to the front garden and we leave a chair positioned so that Reggie can sit and watch any comings and goings. Beagles hate to be left (which doesn't seem fair considering how much they love running off) and we try to include them as much as possible in any activity, even if it's just the school run – they would rather be in the car than home alone. Sometimes, however, it is necessary to go out without beagles in tow, and every time, Reggie will take up his position on the chair, glowering as we walk past the window to walk down the drive or get into the car. We return to Reggie's stern, disapproving face at the window, but this soon turns to ecstatic joy in the form of his welcome routine. Little Hec joins in the homecoming celebrations with a lovely display of play fighting. Reggie's perfect day is when all seven of us are at home. Then he can relax.

While we knew that there would be many more beagley adventures with double the number of beagles, particularly since one has a disability, we could never have predicted the scrapes they get into and the chaos they cause.

THREE

Railway Beagles

The day started perfectly normally. It was a warm summer's day and I dropped Freddy off at school with the beagles in the back of the car. I continued on to the marshes, a beautiful piece of countryside on the River Yare just south of Norwich. The marshes are a dog walker's paradise: they are safe, with no roads in sight, and dogs can have a wonderful run over a wide area of marshland, fields and woods. Reggie, Hector and I set off: Reg in the lead, Hec in hot pursuit and me bringing up the rear with the buggy. We met Jango with Katie-Jango in tow and set off on our usual circular walk. Reggie, as has been mentioned more than once, has a mind of his own and likes to do his own thing, often disappearing for ten or twenty minutes into the undergrowth, but always popping up somewhere along the line and finding us.

That day, Reggie did his usual slipping-off when I was mid-conversation, but this time Hector went with him. This was far more worrying since the marshes are criss-crossed with dykes and rivulets and Hector can't swim. It's difficult to swim with only three legs and even if he did manage it, he wouldn't be able to haul himself out, up the steep, slippery banks. After they had been out of sight for around half an hour I really started to worry. We looked all over, but a lot of the marshes aren't really accessible to people, being much more suited to deer, rabbits, or dogs. After around an hour, Katie had to go as she had an appointment, but she didn't want to abandon me with the beagles still missing and I had to insist. Twenty minutes later (still no sign of the beagles), Katie-Jango returned with a bottle of water and a bagel for me – I had already been out for around two and a half hours, and she wanted to make sure that I at least had provisions before heading off. Katie also checked the main road for any sign of them and phoned to confirm that they were at least not scampering down the A140.

So I stood and I stood. Many dog walkers came past. All said they would keep their eyes peeled for the missing beagles, and many took my phone number in case they spotted them. As time went on, the worry and stress levels rising (by this stage, I had given up worrying about the work that I wasn't doing and focused all my worry on the dogs), a couple of marshes regulars offered to go in different directions – one checking the nearby allotments, another the woods. I felt absolutely helpless, but was sure that I should stay in the area where I had last seen them – dogs have a knack of finding their way back to the same place, and if I moved I felt I may never find them, nor them me.

Kate, a lady I had chatted to in the park on a couple of occasions, arrived for her walk with Millie (sweet blue roan cockapoo). She heard the story, promised to keep her eyes peeled and headed off towards the river. When Kate and Millie reached the corner, where I could just about still see them, Kate shouted and waved excitedly at me. I raced over, dragging the buggy, and strained to spot Reggie as she pointed at a place deep in the distance. Eventually, I saw the unmistakable white tip of a beagle tail streaking along the field, and a feeling of huge relief swept over me – Reggie was alive. The relief was pretty short-lived, however, since there was no sign of Hector... plus the field was across the other side of the river and the only place I knew to cross was about a mile away in the opposite direction to which Reggie was running.

Reggie suddenly stopped and looked in our direction. As he caught my eye, I could see even from that distance his beagle smile – the innocent "Ah there you are, I'm ready to come now. Got any biscuits?" At first, I couldn't understand why he was running in the wrong direction. He must surely know where to cross the river, and I was preoccupied with the worry of how to find Hector. I imagined him exhausted, unable to keep up with Reggie any longer, however gamely he had tried, lying panting in the long grass. He could be anywhere in about a two-or three-mile radius; and a feeling of dread started to come over me: would we ever be able to find him?

Events unfolded very quickly after that. First, we spotted Hector a couple of hundred metres behind Reg, alternating between quick dashes in Reggie's direction and little lie-downs. I was almost overwhelmed with relief, but in a matter of seconds finally realised why Reggie was running in that direction: there is, in fact, another way across the river – over the railway bridge – that is to say, a bridge over which trains travel – not one meant for dogs or people! Reggie slowed down a bit, got distracted by some important smells, and Hector caught him up. Now they were almost opposite us on the other side of the river and looked pleased to see me. Of course, it wasn't possible to explain to them that they must not cross the railway bridge. It is only a branch line, so trains are relatively infrequent and are fairly small, but there are trains. We often see and hear them on our walks. There was nothing for it – I would have to try to get onto the bridge from our side and catch them before they got onto the railway tracks.

Kate and I ran over to the fence, both shouting in the panic of it all. Then Kate pointed again and said in a surprisingly low voice, "Look, they're on the bridge..." I froze for a second as the full horror of the situation sunk in. Suddenly, a young chap rushed over on his bike to see what the commotion was all about. He arrived just as I was hauling myself over the fence and seeing the empty buggy next to a deep fast-flowing river, leapt off his bike ready to jump in and rescue what he, quite understandably, thought must be a baby or small child. I could hear Kate quickly explaining the situation, and without a moment's hesitation, the young man had jumped over the fence, overtaken me and was storming through the four-foot nettles and matted thorn bushes in his shorts, every few seconds calling back to me to see if I was okay.

"Thank you so much," I puffed. "Are you okay with bare legs?"

"Yes, absolutely fine. I've just got back from Zambia – a few nettles don't bother me. My name's Sam – what about you?"

"Victoria," I panted. "Can you get through?"

"Yes, I used to play down here when I was little – I know the way – just follow me!" Sam called.

We both carried on through the undergrowth, Sam having made a bit of a path for me to follow.

The lush green foliage of Marston Marshes both hampered our progress and blocked our view. I didn't dare hope that the dogs had carried on walking over the bridge in our direction and were safely snuffling about in the bushes.

"I can see them again now; they're still on the bridge – they haven't moved," said Sam.

I looked up and there were Reggie and Hector, panting hard, standing on the railway bridge, the other side of the river from us. Reg was looking around, and I started to shout his name furiously. I saw his ears prick up as he looked about, and he started to come across the bridge following the direction of my voice, with Hector hopping slowly behind him, clearly exhausted. Then there was a tingling, which rapidly become a rattling noise and Sam shouted, "There's a train coming." The beagles were almost exactly halfway across the bridge – in other words, it was just as far to get off from either direction.

"Stop calling them," shouted Sam. The rattling and clattering was loud now, and I could see the train approaching across a distant field. In a flash, it was nearly upon us, and I was rooted to the spot in panic. Sam shouted, struggling to make himself heard above the noise, "Victoria – close your eyes! I'm closing mine." I closed my eyes and held onto a branch of a tree next to me. The train roared across the bridge and on top of the deafening clattering noise, blasted its horn. I stood completely still with my eyes tightly shut, listening to the train as it rattled off into the distance and quiet returned to the marshes.

The silence was broken by Sam shouting, "They're okay –Victoria – they're okay – look!"

I opened my eyes to see Reggie and Hector still standing stock-still halfway across the bridge. I shouted to them and saw their tails starting to wag.

Within the space of a few moments, Sam had scaled the escarpment and was on the bridge scooping up Hector under his arm and telling Reggie to come.

Sam carried Hector down from the bridge and all the way through the undergrowth back to where I was standing, with Reg following at his heels. I hugged both the dogs and with trembling fingers managed to put Reg's lead on. Sam carried Hector back to where Kate was waiting with Millie and the buggy, tears of joy and relief in her eyes. We both hugged Sam, who brushed it all off. "And I thought Norwich was going to be a bit tame after Zambia," he grinned, "not a bit of it!"

What a day! Kate kindly wrestled Hector into the buggy and walked back to the car park with me. We got the beagles into the back of the car and with some relief shut the door. Kate asked if I was okay to drive after all the trauma, to which I replied that I was fine.

It was some months later when recounting the tale that Kate mentioned she had turned back after we had said goodbye, and I had sat down on the ground with my head in my hands – probably as the full horror hit home of what would have happened if they had been on the other track. I finally made it home – our walks are normally about an hour or an hour and a half, and I had been out for four! My phone had about ten messages from all the wonderful dog walkers at the marshes, who had taken my number in case they had spotted the beagles. I called them all back one by one and told them a short version of the tale. All dog lovers, they were absolutely horrified by the story, but "All's well that ends well" was how most people put it before they said goodbye.

As for Reggie and Hector: well, they were not affected in any way, shape or form – just a bit tired. It really must have been petrifying to have been so close to a train moving at speed – the noise alone must have been incredible. But, of course, dogs (even Reggie!) would have no idea of the danger that they had been in and what would have happened if they had been on the other track. I'm glad that they are blissfully ignorant of this, and really all they will ever worry about is when the next walk is and where the next biscuit is coming from.

The spot on the marshes where Kate had waited while the terrible sequence of events unfolded has ever since been known as 'Reggie Corner'.

FOUR

Hector's Wheels

Hector's 'good leg' was showing more and more signs of strain. Luckily a small beagle (as opposed to Reg, who is an extra-large one), Hector was now fully grown and pretty sturdy. We tried our hardest to limit his food for his own good, but the combination of his greed, our soft hearts and less exercise than a four-legged dog would have, meant that Hector was prone to getting a bit podgy. Clearly, putting him in a baby's buggy when tired on the walk could only be a short-term solution and wouldn't give him the exercise he desperately needed – we needed to find a way to preserve his 'good leg'. If his other front leg ended up buckling under the strain and he was left with only his two working back legs, it would be a very bad state of affairs for Hector.

I remembered a friend telling me once that she had found goose nappies on the internet when she had rescued a poor lost gosling on the River Thames:

"You can get absolutely everything in America, you know," she had said. Yes, she had actually ordered 'goose diapers' from America and not only that, but had put them on the unsuspecting gosling and presumably changed its nappies on a regular basis!

I started to search the internet for solutions and very soon established that carts, or doggy wheelchairs, can be specially made. Now I was getting somewhere. There are several companies which make such contraptions, but they are all for dogs with back leg trouble. The reason for this is that many of our much-loved dogs have problems with their hips in later life (rather like humans, in fact) and there are various chariots which can be found to keep them mobile. But nothing for a dog with a missing or injured front leg. Nothing at all. Then, finally, an American company, 'Eddie's Wheels', came up, which actually specialised in wheelchairs for dogs (and other animals) with missing or injured *front* legs. I showed James, who is an engineer, and he agreed that the wheelchairs looked really well designed and we should contact the company. The idea of having a wheelchair specially made for Hector in Massachusetts and shipped over to Norwich seemed preposterous at first. We had no idea what it might cost, but when we received the quote we were actually pleasantly surprised – for something that would transform Hector's life, it was worth every cent. We didn't hesitate.

We were sent a diagram showing the very numerous and precise measurements that needed to be taken. Lucky we had an engineer in the family as it was quite a challenge! James and Ellie (a budding engineer) stood Hector on the garden table for a long and complex session of measuring, which also involved a good number of dog treats at regular intervals. They spent a great deal of time checking and rechecking the figures – the idea of having something made to the wrong specification and then shipped from the States was horrifying! After many emails backwards and forwards between Massachusetts and Norwich, the wheelchair company was happy with the measurements we had given them and the work to build Hector's wheels began. The household was lifted by a positive energy – it was incredibly exciting – but would it actually work?

A few weeks later the wheels arrived. It was a monumental and much-anticipated day in late June. We waited until James was home as some assembly was needed, and we couldn't risk getting anything wrong with the precious wheels. It was a fine summer's evening. All were gathered in the garden, the chariot was assembled and Hector's wheels were ready for action. The wheelchair is not unlike a Paralympic racing wheelchair, but with the large, off-road style wheels at the front. Very carefully, James lowered Hector into the wheelchair and strapped him in – his front legs go through some straps and his weight is supported by a webbing cradle under his tummy, with the back legs to be used to propel him forward.

Hector looked confused. It was clear that he wouldn't automatically know what to do and we tried not to be too disappointed. We all called and clapped using high-pitched, excited voices, trying to encourage him to move forward – just a little bit. He wagged his tail and smiled obligingly at all the attention he was getting. Somebody went to get some treats and we laid a trail in front of him. "Come on, Hector. Come and get them!" But he had no idea how he could possibly move in the aluminium frame we had put him in and clearly would have had no idea why we would have done such a thing. Hector stayed put and Reg hoovered up all the treats. It really wasn't working – we were all deflated and disappointed. We took Hector out of the wheels, gave him a few biscuits to help get over his traumatic experience and gave up for the day.

Every day we tried to teach Hector to move in his wheels. We tried some of his absolute favourite snacks – cheddar cheese, sausages, ham; but nothing worked. We looked on the American website for any tips and were reassured to read that most dogs take some while to learn how to use their wheelchair and that much perseverance and patience were needed. It was Max who had the breakthrough. He put Hec in the wheels before his breakfast and then put a trail of warm sausage on the lawn. Hector strained forward, his big black beagle button nose flaring at the sausage smells, and he propelled himself forward the few centimetres needed to reach the first treat. He gobbled that one up and moved on to the next – now he was getting the hang of it, but I don't think he even noticed; such was the intent focus on getting to the warm sausage. Every day, we had a dedicated training session in the garden, and Hector learned to push himself along in the wheels – success!

We went away for a weekend and left Reggie and Hector with Beagle-Emma and full instructions about the wheels. We had started to take the wheels on walks with us but just ended up carrying them as well as Hector (extremely awkward) as Hector only shuffled along very slowly a few centimetres at a time, which really didn't work on a dog walk. Emma, who likes a challenge, particularly when beagles are involved, tried a new tactic on the walk: she let him run free to start with, then put him in the wheels when he was tired. This worked really well, and by the time we got home, Hector was able to propel himself in his wheels at speed. How fantastic! We would now be able to do so many things with Hector that had previously been impossible – simple things such as walking Freddy to school – Hector would be able to walk with Reg without struggling and making his good leg worse. This was the whole point.

With the new-found freedom of the wheels, things were greatly improved, but it wasn't all plain sailing. Reg would pull on the lead and Hector was fairly slow to start with, so I would have my arms fully outstretched in opposite directions, each beagle pulling and straining. Going off-road, Hector would often take a corner too sharply and 'turn turtle' – he would be helplessly marooned on his back, his three legs flailing as he would struggle to right himself. This was a pitiful sight! He couldn't possibly right himself, and we would rush over to help him – this was okay as long as he was in view, but once he was in long grass and we couldn't see him, it was tricky! We would call and call and he wouldn't make a sound – we couldn't understand it! Surely he must realise that he needs to communicate with us in order to be rescued? But he always remained silent and would therefore sometimes be marooned for many minutes before we finally found him, righted the chariot and set him on his way. I mentioned what we thought was

Hector's complete stupidity to dog-trainer-Jacquie, and she explained that dogs can't bark when they are on their back – it's a physical impossibility. So now we knew.

Walking along the pavement to school, or on our way to the park, people would stop and point. On several occasions, the traffic stopped while the passengers in all the cars pointed incredulously at Hector. Even more than before, people would stop and ask us what had happened to Hector, and we would tell his story. Hector became An Even Better Known Local Dog.

The wheels are such a clever bit of engineering. They look just like a simple frame, but a dog can pretty much do anything in them and they are specially designed so that both number ones and number twos are no problem. It's one thing for passing traffic to see a dog trundling along happily in a wheelchair, and it's another for them to see a wheelchair-bound beagle having a poo on the side of the road! In his wheels, Hector can go up and down hills, through rough terrain and shallow water – he literally knows no bounds!

"Hector's just been on BBC Radio Norfolk!" A friend rang to say, "There was a phone-in about what makes people happy, and someone rang to say the little beagle that they see in a wheelchair walking through Norwich always lifts their spirits!" A neighbour went on a training course and each person in the group had to talk about something positive they had seen or done that week: a woman talked about the little dog on wheels she had seen the day before. Little children would point and say, "Look, Mummy – there's Wheelie Dog." A lady got off her bike, crossed the road and came over to say, "I love seeing your dog in his wheels – it gives us all hope."

After a couple of months, Hector was an absolute whizz on his wheels. He could turn on a sixpence, and he could power along at a great rate of knots, almost keeping up with Reggie and only being thwarted by natural barriers such as streams or hedges, or man-made ones like steep steps or fences. He learned to judge the width of gateways and could manoeuvre himself through a stile as long as someone held the gate open. It was a joy to watch him belting along with the other dogs in the park, often doing his 'squeaky wheel' hunting cry as he went, which is quite ironic considering that he is a dog on wheels. People had really never seen anything like it, and they never stopped telling us so! Walking with Hector in his wheels on the lead is never particularly straightforward. When a beagle sniffs the ground, it's almost like an anteater, thrusting the snout into the grass with a swift and sudden movement. This is exaggerated severalfold when your beagle is in wheels, as it stops dramatically, often right in your path, and a dog in wheels forms a far more solid barrier than a dog without wheels – meaning the person on the

other end of the lead will go head over heels if they
don't have their wits fully about them. Hector takes
sniffing particularly seriously, with the sniff going
through his entire body, all the while making a bizarre
Darth Vader-like breathing noise.

FIVE

Reggie Island

After school drop-off, I drove to the marshes and met Beagle-Emma. The beagles galloped off in their usual excited frenzy, with Hector bringing up the rear in his wheels. There is a man-made path around the marsh, with the river on one side and a very smart golf course on the other. Water is the main hazard, and while the frame for Hector's wheels is super-light, the wheels are solid and, clearly, deep water is very dangerous for Hector. The 'interior' of the marsh, which is what I call the large central area off the path, is a minefield of deep ditches and water-filled dykes and very long grass, with rough, bumpy ground – not at all ideal for Hector.

The beagles were all ahead of us on that cold, grey November morning, and Emma and I marched along behind them, stamping in our wellies to keep warm. Deep in conversation, we didn't notice at first that Reggie had peeled off the path and was heading silently into the interior. In fact, we only noticed when we realised that Hector was in hot pursuit, shrieking as he went – the hunt was on! I ran after Hector to try to grab him before he entered the hazardous interior, but he was like a dog possessed and flew along over the rough terrain at an incredible rate – I couldn't catch him. By this time, I was some way into the interior myself; Beagle-Emma had managed to put Bo and Roxy on their leads and was making her way over to help. I could keep track of Reggie for a while, following the white tip of his tail as it streaked through the long grass, but had lost sight of Hector. This was a major worry – if he fell into any of the deep dykes in his wheels, he would have absolutely no chance of getting out. V-shaped, with steeply sloping sides, even a fully able dog without wheels would find it hard to climb out of one of those dykes. A feeling of foreboding started to come over me – I couldn't see him anywhere.

Emma reached me and suggested that we went towards the spot where I had last seen Reggie – Hector would be following him and we were bound to find him on the way – probably stuck on a tree root or turned over in his wheels and unable to alert us as to his whereabouts. We trekked across the rough ground, calling Reggie and Hector constantly. We then happened upon the wheels – with no Hector. From the evidence in front of us we could deduce that Hector had indeed turned turtle and had somehow managed to wriggle out of his wheels altogether.

So now Hector was at large in the interior with no wheels, which was good and bad. Good as there would be less chance of drowning (although we really thought he couldn't swim) and bad because he could get so exhausted that he would just lie down and wait to be rescued and we might not be able to find him.

Emma suddenly pointed and said, "I can see Reggie – look; he's right over there!" We rushed in that direction; I was carrying the wheels, Emma with Bo and Roxy. But we were cut off by a dyke – Reggie was on the other side. We followed the dyke for a while, the feeling of panic rising more and more – where was Hector? We then heard a distant squeaky wheel noise – not only was he alive, but he was in hot pursuit of some prey! Now we just needed to find him – the noise was coming from the other side of the water. We called and called while walking along, trying to find an end to the dyke, and finally it dawned on us that the dogs must be on an island. Things were going from bad to worse. We walked and walked and walked, but there was no end to the dyke – as we had feared, it was indeed an island. I had no worries about Reg – he is a good swimmer and fit and strong – crossing the dyke wouldn't be a problem for him. But Hector? How had he got on the island in the first place? Now we could hear no noises and we could see no beagles… we were looking and listening and suddenly we heard a loud splash – just as if someone or something had fallen or jumped into the water.

"Oh, my goodness, Victoria, that could be Hector falling in," exclaimed Beagle-Emma. "What are we going to do?" There was silence from the island. "I'm going across," she said. "He could be drowning!"

Taking my winter coat off, I said, "No, Emma, if anyone has to go in, it has to be me – he's my dog!" I hesitated for a couple of seconds, looking at the black, freezing water and wondering how deep it was… and what might lie beneath the ominous-looking surface. With that, I hurled myself into the dyke, shrieking with distress and cold and fear. I immediately realised that my phone was in my jeans pocket, managed to fish it out and throw it to Emma while treading water. I got across to the other side of the bank, which wasn't at all far, wailing continuously and then wailed even louder with frustration when I realised that there was absolutely no way I could climb out. The sides were almost vertical; the thick, dark mud was as slippery as wet clay, and there was simply nothing to grab hold of. Desperate clutches at clumps of long grass just gave me handfuls of grass and nothing to grip. Every second was another that Hector could be drowning, and rather than saving him, I was completely stuck. I had one last attempt to push myself up onto the bank, using all the strength I could possibly muster – but it was no good; I just slid back down, plopping back into the water. The situation was grim. I wailed some more and rested my head on the muddy bank for a few seconds, trying to decide what to do next.

All at once, I felt hot breath against my cheek, followed by a piercing beagle-cry right down my ear, and there was Hector! He was alive and very well and was presumably wondering what all the wailing was about! Not only was he alive, but he seemed absolutely delighted with himself, hopping about and whooping to his heart's content. I grabbed hold of him and Emma shouted: "I'll throw you the lead. Clip him on and I'll drag him across!" It would have been fairly tricky for me to get across the dyke, carrying Hector as I swam in full clothes (including wellies; I hadn't taken them off). This seemed like a good plan, and I clipped the lead on to Hector's collar. On the count of three, I almost threw him across the water, with Emma reeling him in like a large flappy salmon. He made it and now it was a question of my getting back to the other bank. "I'm going to throw you two leads," called Emma, "grab hold of them and I'll drag you across too!" Spiderman-esque, Emma flung out a lead from each hand across the dyke. I managed to catch them and holding one in each hand, again on the count of three, hurled myself across the water and with Emma pulling, made it to the bank. The final step was Emma pulling me out, which took all her strength and determination and was accompanied by a lot of shouting from both of us. She pulled so hard that as I slithered up the near-vertical mud wall, Emma fell backwards, splat on her bottom in the deep, slightly smelly black mud.

So Beagle-Emma was sitting in the mud and I was lying in it, covered from the neck down in black slime, while Hector, Bo and Roxy were jumping around excitedly, with plenty of mud on them too. The situation, while not exactly perfect, had certainly improved in that it was no longer life-threatening at least. All we needed now was for Reg to turn up. On cue, he appeared on the far bank and not wanting to miss out on all the fun, proceeded to leap into the water, doggy-paddle deftly across the dyke, and come to join in.

Surprisingly (it was November), I really didn't feel that cold – fear and adrenalin have an amazing effect on the human body. We trudged back to the cars – which is quite a long way with your wellies full of water – bumping into various dog walkers who, by the state of our little party, were quick to work out at least roughly what had happened. Emma gave me a plastic bag so that I had something to sit on in the car and phoned James, who was working from home that day, saying "I think you had better run a bath; Victoria's been for a bit of a swim."

When I got home, I took off my slime-covered clothes at the back door – there were rotten black leaves down the leg of my jeans and various clumps of sludge under my jumper. It was only then that I started to feel a bit chilly. I had the bath that had been run, but then had to have a shower afterwards on account of the bath water being polluted by black slime. Meanwhile, James washed the beagles, and after a hot cup of coffee, normality was restored.

"There's an island at the marshes, you know," I said to James. "It's called Reggie Island."

Abandoned Beagle

I looked on my phone: nine missed calls from unknown numbers and seven voicemails…

I was in London for a work meeting; and when we stopped for a coffee break, I glanced at my phone – I couldn't believe what I saw! I immediately thought that Ellie, Max or Freddy had been in an accident and, taking deep breaths, I stepped outside the building to listen to the voicemails:

"Hello, hi, can you hear me okay? I've found your dog, at the UEA lake – please call when you get this message."

"Hello, it's me, Steve, again. I don't know if you got my last message, but I've still got your dog – Hector. Please give me a ring back."

"Hi – I don't think you can be receiving my messages… I found your dog Hector – a beagle – tied to a bench at the UEA lake. Hope to hear from you."

"Hello – Steve here. Listen, I have to go. I'll have to take your dog to security. Please call."

"Hi – I've taken Hector to the security office at UEA – they said they would look after him until you get there. Sorry, but I couldn't wait any longer."

Well, I couldn't imagine what had happened. There were two more messages. These were from Granny:

"I had lost Hector, well, and Reggie too for that matter, but apparently someone has taken him to the security office and I'm going to collect him now."

"Panic over! Hector and Reggie are both safe and sound and we're going home now. See you later!"

At least, by the time I had listened to the last message, I knew that both beagles were safe and well. But I couldn't imagine what on earth had happened, so I phoned Steve (a complete stranger) and then Granny and was able to piece together the order of events from what they both told me.

When I have to go to London or away somewhere for work, Super Granny sweeps into the house and looks after everything with endless energy and impressive efficiency. My mother-in-law really is a proper 'Super Granny' and by this I mean that not only does she lead a full and active life and looks after Grandpa, who has a long-term illness, but she plays a big part in the lives of all her eight grandchildren. Granny has helped look after my children ever since they were babies. Not only that, but she also looks after Reggie and Hector every time we go on holiday as well as various other family dogs.

I took an early train to London. After getting the children off to school, Granny took the dogs for a walk to Eaton Park and beyond to the UEA lake. UEA stands for the University of East Anglia, which has extensive grounds where lots of people walk their dogs on a circular route around the lake. Granny had taken Reggie and Hector on this walk several times before, and while I wouldn't claim that all walks are incident-free, nothing could have prepared poor Granny for the traumatic episode that unfolded that morning.

On one side of the lake there is a large expanse of grass, which slopes up to the university buildings on top of the hill. There are woods to one side and thick, wild undergrowth to the other. Stay on the path and you have a lovely, civilised walk; stray into the undergrowth and you don't know what you may find – squirrels, rabbits, deer – the possibilities are endless, or so thinks Reg. Reggie took off into the undergrowth, clearly on an exciting and unmissable scent, and Hector careered after him in his wheels. Now, the wheels are robust and they are very much off-road by design, but they are not built to plough successfully through thickets of hawthorn, intertwined with any number of other wild, scrubby and thorny plants.

The scene was chaotic: the disabled beagle in his wheelchair, squeaky wheel hunting cry, careering at full pelt, with Granny in hot pursuit through the dense undergrowth. Granny didn't get very far, and soon Hector was out of sight and earshot. So Granny did what we normally do in these situations: sat tight and waited in the place where we last saw the dogs, calling occasionally... they would come back eventually, they always do. But they didn't. There was no sign. Granny felt she should start walking and asked every dog walker she met if they had seen any sign of either Reggie or Hector. Several people knew the dogs, or if they didn't actually know them, had seen Hector around, so they all knew what they were looking for – many kind dog walkers took Granny's number in case they spotted them.

After about forty-five minutes, Super Gran, who is super-cool in all situations, was starting to panic. The problem once again was water: what if Hector had somehow fallen in the lake or one of the surrounding dykes in his wheels and had drowned? At her wit's end and not knowing what to do next, Granny saw a man approaching with a large white husky dog and what appeared to be Hector under his arm. Yes, it was Hector – he was soaking wet and covered in mud, so now his rescuer Bob was also wet and muddy.

Hector was pleased to see Granny, who almost wept with relief: Reg would be okay. At least Hector was safe and well, but it had been a very close-run thing. Bob had been one of the people Granny had spoken to when she was searching for the dogs, so he and Oz the husky had gone off purposefully to see if they could find the beagles. Walking along the path, Oz had suddenly darted off and started to bark furiously. Bob made his way to where Oz was barking and saw Hector floundering in a dyke, struggling to keep his head above water and then sinking right under. Without a moment's hesitation, Bob waded into the dyke and fished Hector out, literally saving his life. He then, despite the fact that he walks with a stick, carried the exhausted and traumatised Hector all the way along the path until he found Granny.

"I can't thank you enough," exclaimed Granny,

"but did you see any sign of the wheels?" Bob knew Hector and had often seen him in his wheels, but no, he hadn't seen them. This was a major problem – the wheels are Hector's lifeline and came custom-made all the way from America. They could be anywhere in the vast expanse of the UEA grounds. What was Granny to do? Bob and Oz went in one direction, taking Granny's number and promising to call if they found them. Granny looked at Hector – he was beat – he couldn't walk another step... but Granny wouldn't be able to search far and wide for the all-important wheels while carrying the very stocky, weighty Hector, not to mention the fact that he was black with mud. So Granny tied Hector to one of the benches by the lake, making sure that he had plenty of room on the lead to lie down and rest. She then headed off in the opposite direction to Bob in search of the wheels. The normally ever-optimistic Granny held out little hope of finding them – the task was virtually impossible, but she had to try...

Steve-the-dog-walker came along the path by the lake with the four dogs he regularly walks as his job. At the sight of four dogs approaching, Hector leapt up and started to howl, and what a pitiful sight it was! A small, disabled beagle, soaking wet and covered in mud, was tied to a park bench – abandoned! Steve came over to Hector and patted him reassuringly, telling him not to worry. He saw a mobile number on Hector's tag and left a message:

"Hello, hi, can you hear me okay? I've found your dog, at the UEA lake – please call when you get this message."

When no one called him back, he left four further messages. Still no reply. So he carried Hector in his arms, somehow holding four dog leads, up the long slope to the top of the hill where the university buildings are. Asking a passer-by, he was directed to the security office, where he left Hector.

Meanwhile, Super Granny was rushing along the path looking out for the wheels and calling Reggie. When Reggie popped out of the undergrowth, panting and exhausted, Granny was understandably elated. Putting Reggie on a lead and scolding him absent-mindedly– "Reggie, you ARE a bad dog!" – her mind was fixed on finding those very expensive and absolutely essential wheels. And hey presto – there they were! Up-ended in a blackberry thicket, with thorny branches wrapped round the wheel spokes. Granny managed to free the wheels, and she and Reg went back to find Hector. They reached the bench where Granny had tied him, but there was no sign of him. The lead wasn't there either, so it wasn't that Hector had slipped out of his collar and had escaped; someone must have taken him. Maybe it was the wrong bench. Granny and Reggie checked the next one, but no Hector. A terrible fear overtook poor Granny. There are some awful people around who do dreadful things to animals – no nice person would steal someone else's dog, would they? Granny feared the worst and was at a loss to know what to do next – call the police?

Another dog walker whom Granny had spoken to earlier came over and saved the day. She explained that Steve-the-dog-walker had taken Hector to the security office (she had bumped into him at the time) so he was safe and well. Granny marched up the slope carrying the wheels, with Reggie in tow, and was reunited with Little Hec.

By the time I had come out of my meeting and listened to all the messages, Super Granny, Reggie and Hector were all safely at home. I rang Granny and was given a shortened version of the tale. "But everything's fine now, dear. The doggies are just a bit tired."

"How about you, Granny?" I asked. "You must be exhausted, not to mention traumatised!

"No, I'm absolutely fine, dear. Just getting on with a few shirts. I love ironing, such a nice warm job."

For months afterwards, dog walkers would come

over to me and tell me how they had been at the lake that day and had been involved in the search. And if it hadn't been for the wonderful community of dog walkers in Norwich, particularly fearless Oz and brave Bob, Little Hec wouldn't have lived to tell the tale.

SEVEN

Short Tales

If I were to include all the mini adventures we have ever had, this book would be as long as *Harry Potter and the Deathly Hallows*! So to finish off Hector's story to date, I am going to recount a few short tales that we have found particularly memorable.

C-A-T in the park

Reggie and Hector, while really quite different in character, do have various things in common, such as their enthusiasm for food, their love of radiators and their absolute hatred of cats. One day, on our way home through the park, having had a relatively adventure-free walk so far, we crossed over from the golf course through the car park and into the park. The park is fenced and has a large hedge along the border – on the other side is a fairly busy road. Just as we crossed over from the golf course into the park, Reggie came virtually nose-to-nose with a C-A-T.

Now, as we all know, cats roam about on their own and are very independent of their owners. You often see them round and about, but I don't think cats normally take themselves for walks in the park, do they? Well, Reggie simply couldn't believe it. There was a split second when both cat and beagle froze, and then the cat shot off towards the car park with Reggie hot on its tail and Hector with full volume squeaky wheel behind Reg. The three of them shot past me in a flash of ears, tails, fur and wheels, and I set off in hot pursuit behind Hector.

The cat was clearly heading for home, which meant a dash across the car park (fairly dangerous), followed immediately by a streak across the road (very dangerous) to its own garden, but with the dogs behind it, the poor cat must have panicked, and rather than running straight into its front garden, it turned and started running along the road. I jumped about in the road and managed to stop the oncoming cars – there were several of them. Once the cars had stopped, the situation was greatly improved, and I managed to grab hold of Hec's wheels, got his lead on, handed him quickly to a passing dog walker and went after Reg who was like a cartoon dog, hurling himself against the wooden gate under which the cat had escaped. Yet another near miss for the beagles!

Comedy Baguette

Beagles are quite literally obsessed with food. Here I will introduce two more little-known facts about beagles. First, they have arguably the best nose of all dogs – why then, I hear you cry, are beagles so rarely used as sniffer dogs by police or at airports? Well, having read about Reggie and Hector so far, could you imagine them behaving well enough to perform such important dog duties? They would find suspicious items in a suitcase, there is no doubt about that, but then they would surely dispose of the evidence down their throats! There are exceptions, however, and some very hard-working, well-behaved beagles are out there doing a good job. This brings me to the next point about beagles (also the case with labradors): they have a 'defective' gene, which basically makes them think that they are never full. They will eat pretty much until they burst, if not prevented from doing so, and food has played a key role in many of our adventures.

We were in the park: Jango, Amber, and their humans; Reggie and Hector with theirs. Reggie hared off to the skate park, which is where he displays all the characteristics of an urban hunting beagle. It's his favourite hunting ground for spilt snacks – crisps, biscuits, and if he's really lucky, even the remains of a takeaway can often be found around the skate park area of Eaton Park, particularly first thing in the morning before the rubbish has been collected. On this occasion, it was actually closed for repairs, and the workmen were working away, no doubt looking forward to their lunch break. I tried in vain to call Reggie back – the skate park as a building site was even more interesting than usual, so he had closed his long beagle ears to any boring humans intent on preventing him from finding some tasty snacks.

We stopped a little way away and were debating whether I should go over and try to catch him, when Emma-Amber said, "Look, there he is! He's got something in his mouth – it's quite big – what is that? Oh, I think it's a baguette!"

We watched as Reggie ran off happily with his catch, and I knew that he must have stolen one of the workmen's lunch. I tried to make myself small behind quite a sparse, thin tree, thinking about slinking away without having to admit that he was my dog, when Emma said: "Oh, look now – a man's chasing him, look! He's got a big stick!" And there was Reggie running round and round with the baguette sticking out of his mouth horizontally and a workman in a hard hat and high-vis jacket chasing after him, looking pretty cross, shouting and waving a long pole.

I could no longer hide or slink away: I had to protect Reggie from being whacked by a big stick, however embarrassed I might have been about the sandwich. I walked over to the skate park with trepidation and could see all the other workmen rolling round in laughter, shouting out comments to their mate from time to time. By this point, Reg had got far enough away and we all knew what would have happened to the baguette. Katie-Jango held on to the other dogs, while Emma-Amber and I went over to the poor, lunch-less workman to apologise profusely. Having admitted defeat, the workman was able to join in the laughter with his mates, and after catching the Naughtiest Dog in Norwich, I bought him a replacement lunch, which he accepted with a smile.

Skater Dog

In Eaton Park, I have spent a lot of time in the vicinity of the skate park, Reggie's absolute favourite place for snack-hunting. The skate park is frequented by a variety of children, from tiny tots on three-wheel scooters, to eighteen-year-olds on BMX bikes. There have been lots of times when small children have pointed and said, "Look, Daddy, that doggy's come to the skate park on his wheels!"

Like any other skate park, ours consists of steep-sloped concrete pits – yet another hazard for a dog on wheels. The thought had crossed my mind as to how I could possibly get him out again if Hector wheeled down into one of the pits. The sides are sheer, with nothing to hold on to; it wouldn't be easy. And one day it happened – to the great delight of all children and adults assembled, Hec went too close to the edge of one of the pits when following Reg and accidently and seemingly in slow motion started to wheel down a frighteningly steep drop into a pit. He picked up speed to the bottom and went three quarters of the way up the other side, going back and forth until he finally came to a halt. He looked like he had really enjoyed himself! Fortunately, there were lots of people about – plenty of agile older children who could climb down and push him up the slope – I lay on my belly reaching my arms down and caught hold of the frame of the wheels as he was inched up, and with yet another team effort, one more Hector-rescue was successfully performed.

Reggie Evades Arrest

One Saturday evening we were sitting around the kitchen table with friends, drinking wine and waiting for our takeaway curry to be delivered. The doorbell rang and James went to answer it, armed with cash to pay the delivery man. As is customary when anyone comes to the door, particularly in the dark, there was a chorus of beagle-barking, but it is only in hindsight that I realise it wasn't a chorus at all, just Hector, who is after all the chief guard dog.

James opened the door to a policeman: "Good evening, sir, have you lost a dog?" Confused, James said that we had not, on this occasion, lost one of our dogs. Meanwhile, however, we became aware that Reggie was howling furiously in the *front* garden. Piecing together what must have happened, it went something like this...

Reggie had been making a study of how to open the side gate without anyone noticing. We initially thought that someone must have left it slightly ajar in order for him to escape into the night, but the next day, Reggie forgot himself in the excitement of going on a walk. He revealed his technique, which was a combination of a head-barge to loosen the catch, followed by a clever hooking motion with a front paw. So that's how he had got out. The police patrol car spotted him trotting down one of Norwich's busiest roads, stopped and tried to catch him before he caused an accident. Reggie was having none of it. Ducking and diving and howling, he refused to be caught and took off in the direction of home. The two kind police officers jumped back in the car and trailed him, driving at Reggie-speed a careful distance behind. As Reggie turned into our drive, he about-turned, stood his ground and howled at the now stationary police car, clearly protecting his property. One of the officers skirted round him and came to ring on the doorbell...

James reinforced the catch on the gate.

Not The End

It's hard to know how to finish this story because it hasn't ended! Reggie and Little Hec live with us in Norwich and we go about our daily lives together as a family. A dog on wheels has become so normal for us and for Hector's many friends, both human and canine, that we forget what an unusual sight it actually is. People continue to stop us in the park and on the street, wanting to know Hector's story, and now I've written at least some of it down. As a mature beagle, Hector has become more idiosyncratic, often barking at people for unacceptable behaviour, such as hat-wearing or walking with Nordic ski poles. He's stubborn in the extreme, and if Hector doesn't wish to go, then he does a firm 'heavy dog', almost planting himself into the ground. Coaxing is followed by pathetic pleading, then shouting inevitably follows and I often think how it must look to the passer-by – giving a disabled, wheelchair-bound dog a good dressing down in the street…

The important thing is that Hector lives a happy and fulfilled life. Above all, he is game – he doesn't let his disability get in the way of anything, which is mainly why we have got into so many scrapes! Hector has enriched the lives of his family and friends and gladdens the hearts of the people he meets.

The Kennel Club says, *"The man with the lead in his hand and no dog in sight owns a Beagle"*, so be warned.

Beagles are loving, fun, entertaining medium-sized hounds, but not every household is suited to beagle ownership – a sad fact borne out by the tremendous number of beagles, young and old, who are given up by their owners every day of the year, many of which end up at the Beagle Welfare Trust.

The Beagle Welfare Trust does great work to look after beagles whose owners can no longer do so. As a rough guide, beagles need the following:

A household where they are **not left alone** all day – beagles are pack animals and being left alone for long periods is distressing, resulting in destructive behaviour, which often results in owners giving up their beagles.

A tremendous amount of **exercise**. Beagles are built for stamina, not speed. They would be more than happy to roam absolutely all day. They need a good long walk every day, most preferably off the lead.

A **secure garden.** Beagles are fantastic escapologists.

Relaxed kind-hearted owners, who aren't going to worry much about excellent behaviour – this is rarely achieved in a beagle and if complete control of a dog is what you are after, a beagle is almost certainly not for you.

Love and attention. Beagles are intelligent, they need stimulation, to be in the thick of it; they love nothing more than a game.

10% of the profit made from sales of Hector's Wheels will be donated to The Beagle Welfare Trust.

Stuck again!

Reggie's favourite drinking hole

Sunbathing

Christmas Beagle

Life is good